Tiles of the Alhambra

An Introduction to
Compass and Straight Edge Construction

David Banney

Black Note Press
BCP059
© David Banney, 2020
All rights reserved.
ISBN: 9798715416742

Introduction

Granada in Spain is home to the Alhambra Palace, a ninth century miracle of architecture and design, and home to one of the greatest displays of geometric art. Geometry, based on techniques using compass and straight edge, was brought to an unsurpassed level of sophistication in the cultures of ancient Greece and Persia. The Alhambra receives millions of visitors each year, and many years ago one of these visitors was M.C. Escher, whose extraordinary creations were inspired in large part by the marvels of the Alhambra.

One of the most fascinating aspects of geometry and geometric art is *tessellation*, the art and science of covering a surface without overlaps or gaps. Perhaps the most fascinating examples of tessellation are those that use just a single tile shape – brick walls (using rectangles) and the hexagonal cross section of beehives (hexagons) are well known examples.

This book introduces five tessellating tiles, all of which can be found in the Alhambra Palace, with instructions for their construction using just straight edge and compass. There are many ways to construct each of the tiles, and I have presented just one approach for each one (two approaches in a couple of cases). Each pattern is introduced with an example of a finished tile, as well as an example of the tile in a tessellating pattern.

For each tile there is a diagram showing the basis for the construction of the tile. These tiles can be imagined as 'cutting and pasting' a square or a triangle, and if you are already familiar with compass and straight edge construction, you may wish to find your own approach to constructing the tiles before following my instructions, based on this diagram.

Part of the pleasure of this process is producing the shapes, but the next stage is to produce enough copies to tessellate. This can be done by making one copy and using it as a template, or in a class, each student can produce one copy (ensure that they are the same size by beginning with the same sized circle – there are pages at the back of this book with suitable circles, each marked with a centre point.)

The instructions consist of sequential diagrams that are aimed to be self-explanatory, with little need for a great deal of text. However, two techniques must be learnt before proceeding to the designs: finding the centre of a line and making a right angle (perpendicular) through the centre of a line. These instructions are shown here. Small dots indicate the centre of a circle. Black lines indicate new lines, circles or arcs to be drawn in each step. Dotted lines are the result of previous steps. The final shape is shown in red.

Equipment

You will need:

Compass: A cheap one will get you started, but expect to be frustrated by the inability of a cheap pair of compasses to hold a constant radius.

Pencils and pens: Hard pencils (e.g., 4H) have the advantage of staying sharp longer, and producing fine lines that enhance accuracy, but have the disadvantage of being harder to erase. Soft pencils are easier to erase but go blunt quickly, and bluntness is not good for accuracy. I use a 4H pencil and make the lines and circles as gently as possible. You can use a variety of pens for the final shape, but ensure that the pens that you choose will fit into the compass.

Eraser: A good eraser will give a clean result.

Scissors/knives: How you produce the final tiles is up to you. The tiles can be constructed using paper, cardboard, fridge magnet material, fabric, ceramics, or any other material that you can work with.

How to find the centre of a line

1. Set the compass so that its radius (the distance from the point to the pencil) is more than half the length of the line – the precise radius doesn't matter. Draw two circles of equal radius, using each end of the line as the centre of a circle.

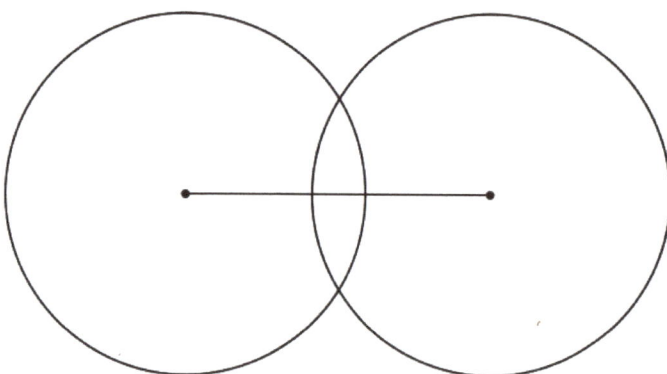

2. Mark the intersection points of the two circles and draw a line that passes through them and through the original line. You have now achieved two things – found the middle of the line, and produced a perpendicular line.

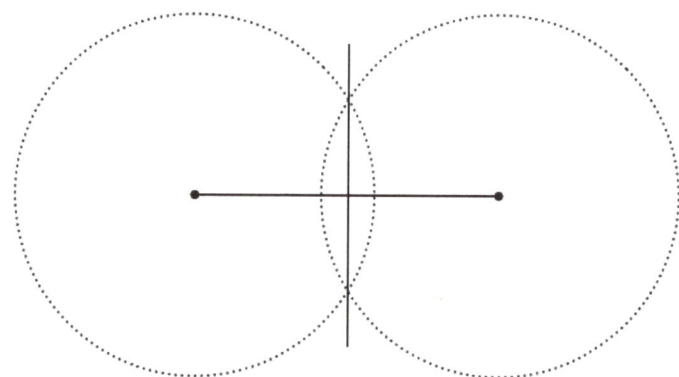

Drawing a square
This technique can be used to produce a square – copy the following sequence of diagrams and repeat the process until you can do it from memory. You will need this technique later.

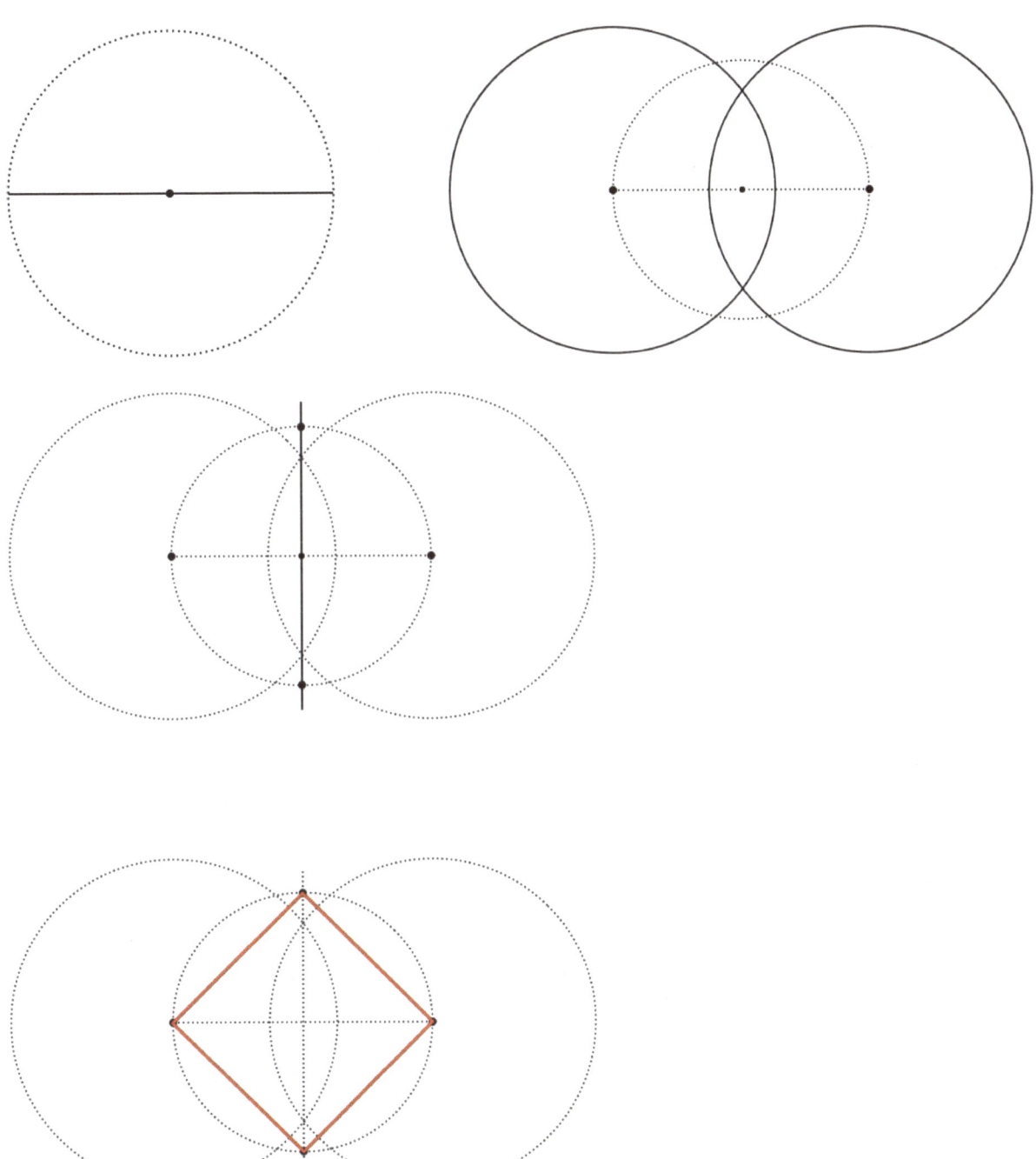

1.

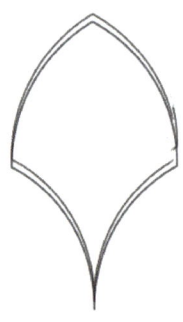

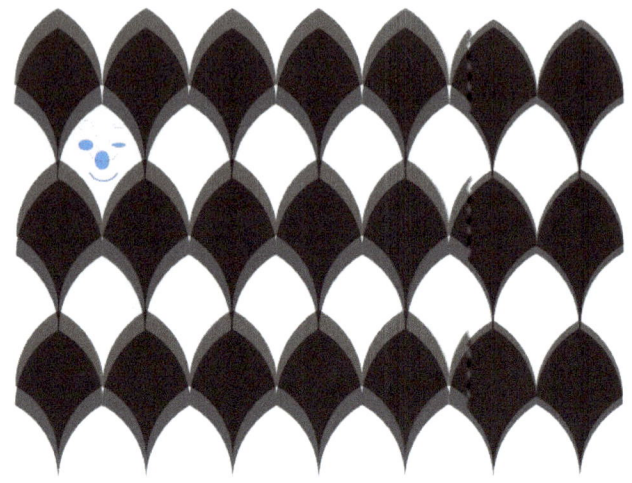

The basis for this tile is a tile constructed from two equilateral triangles, with two segments removed:

However, the tile can be constructed without drawing the triangles, as follows:

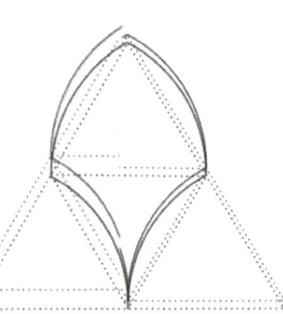

 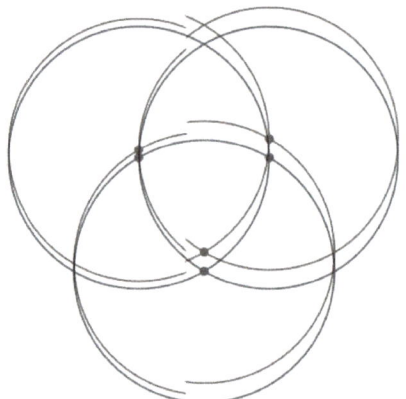

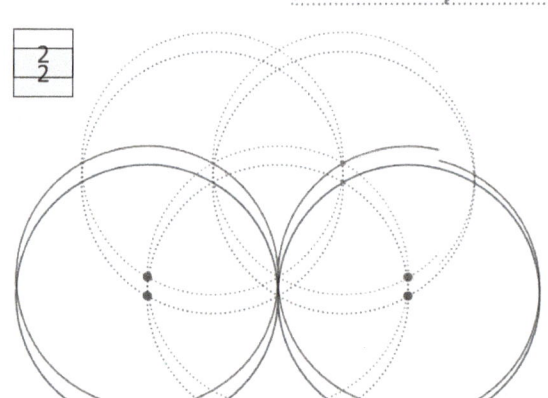

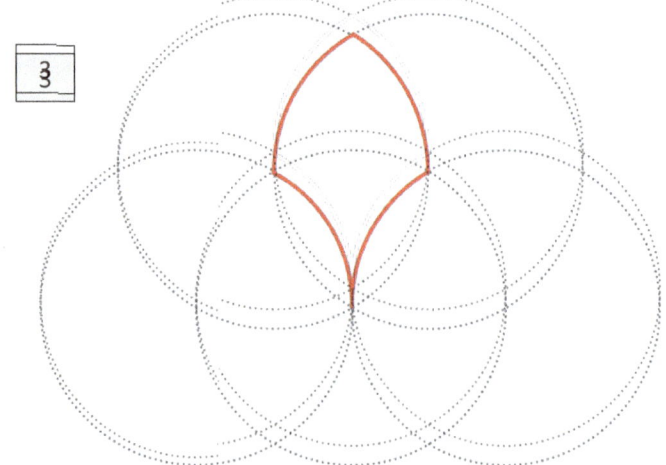

By the way, here are the triangles:

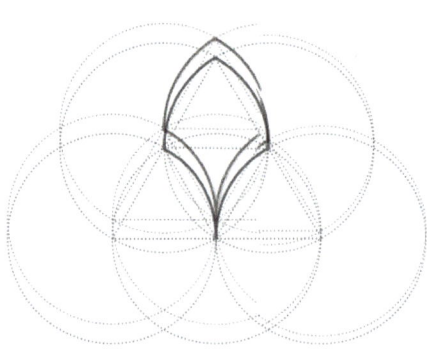

Can you find this tile tessellating in this array of circles? (How would you construct this grid of circles?)

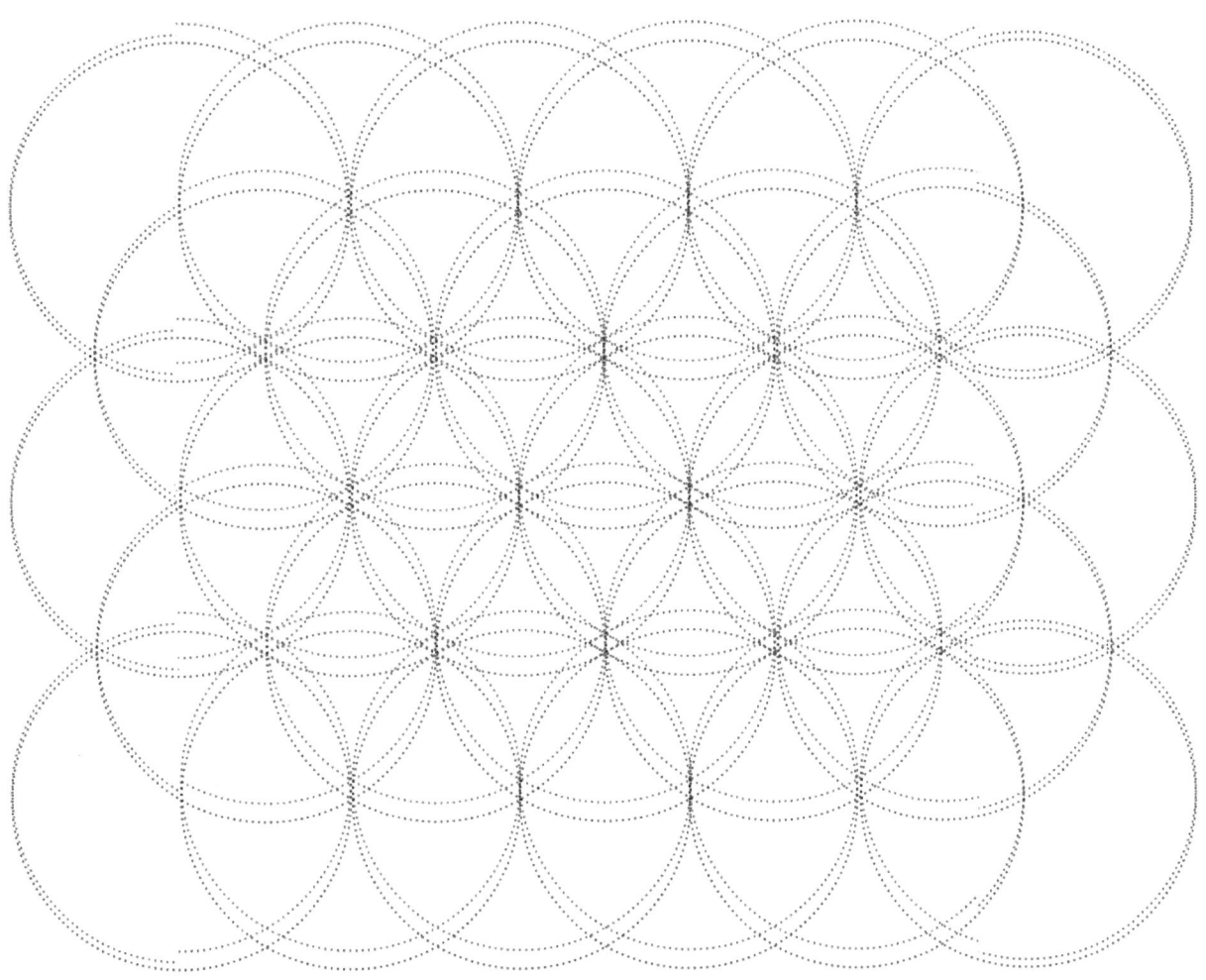

2.

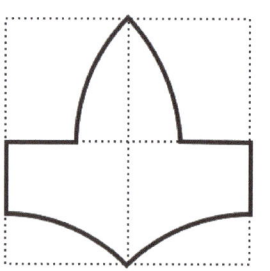

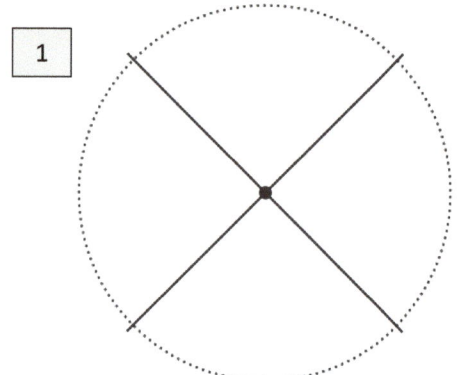

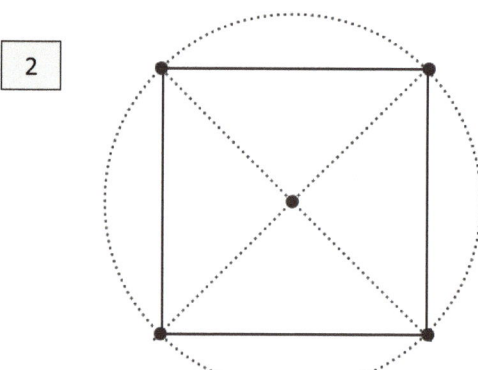

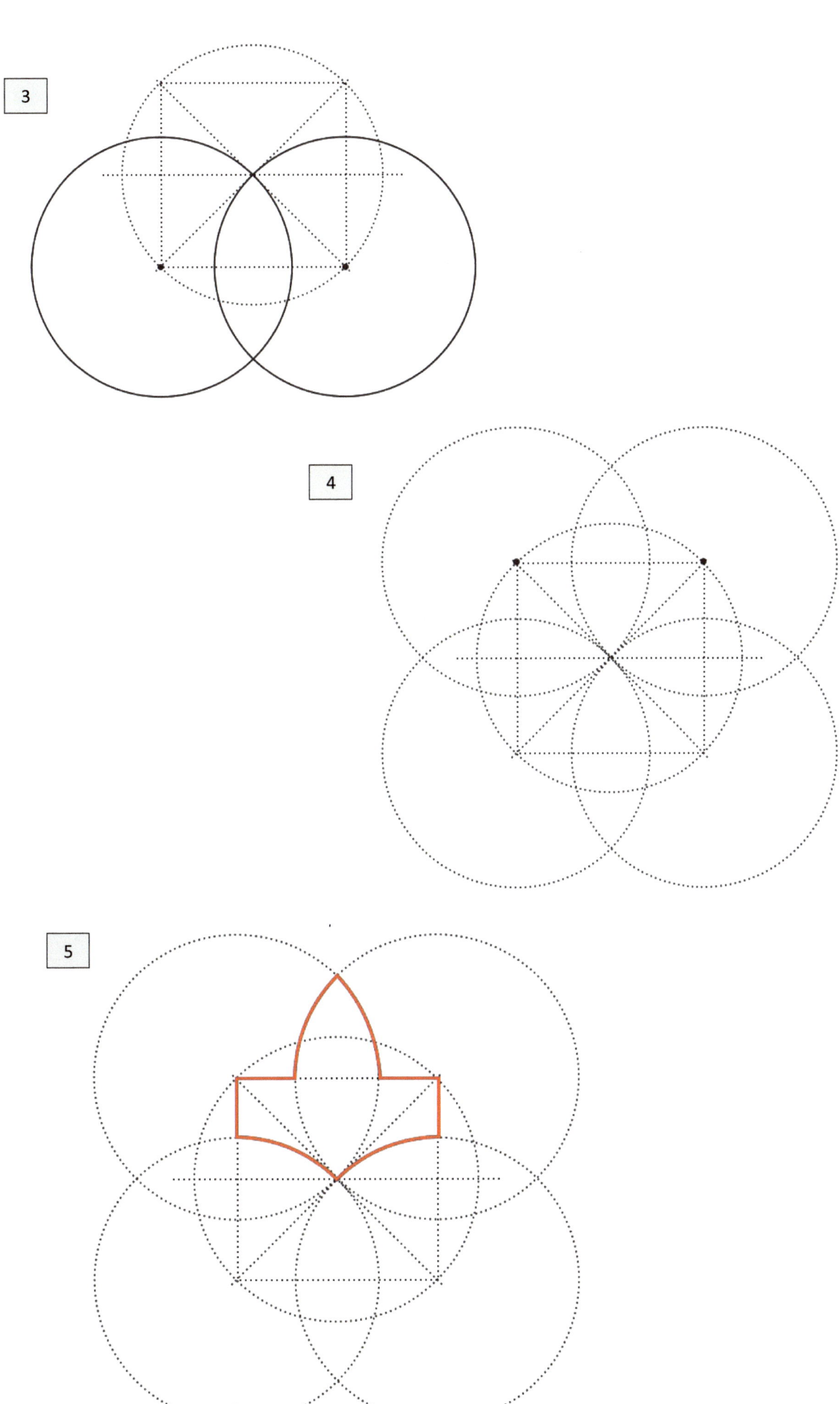

Find this tile tessellating in this grid of circles. (How would you construct this grid of circles?)

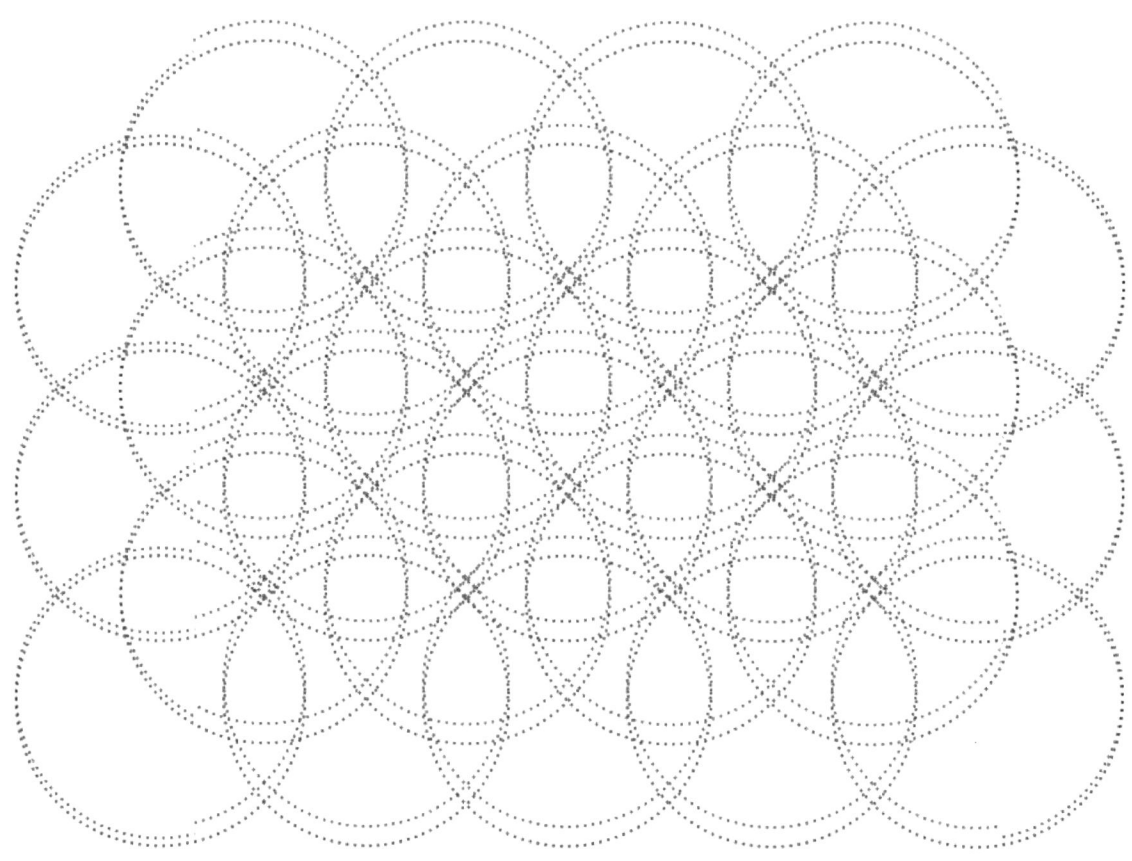

3.

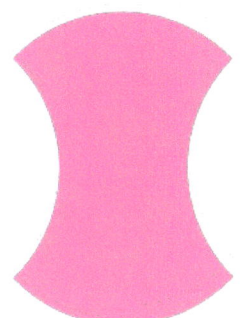
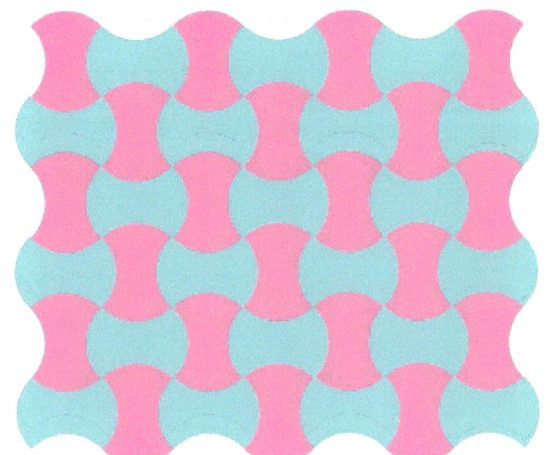

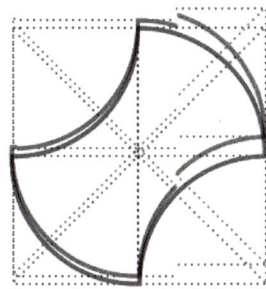

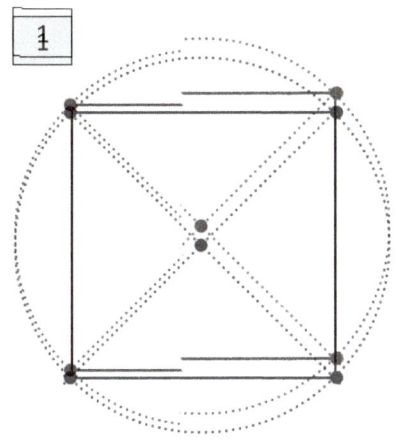
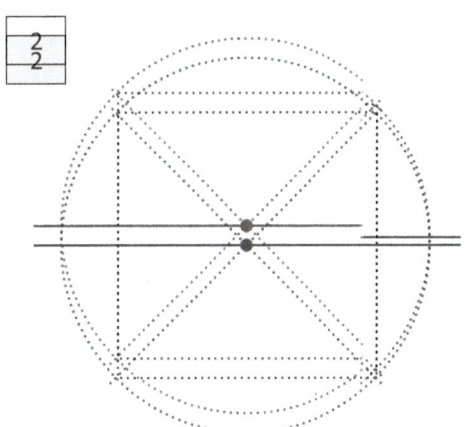

3

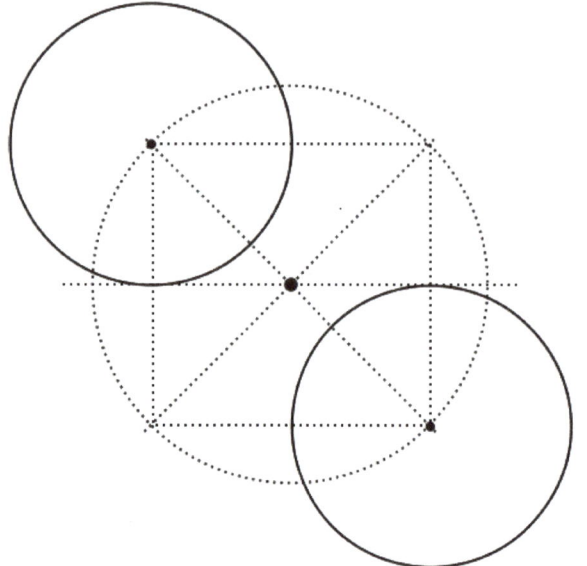

You must reset the radius of the compass for these circles. Use the new radius again in step 4.

4

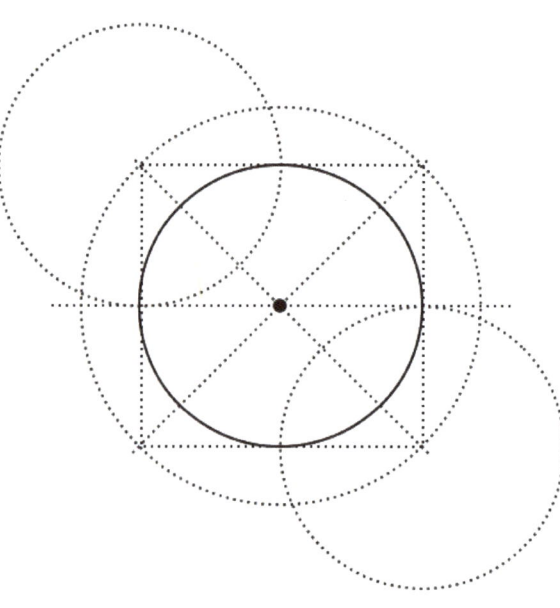

5

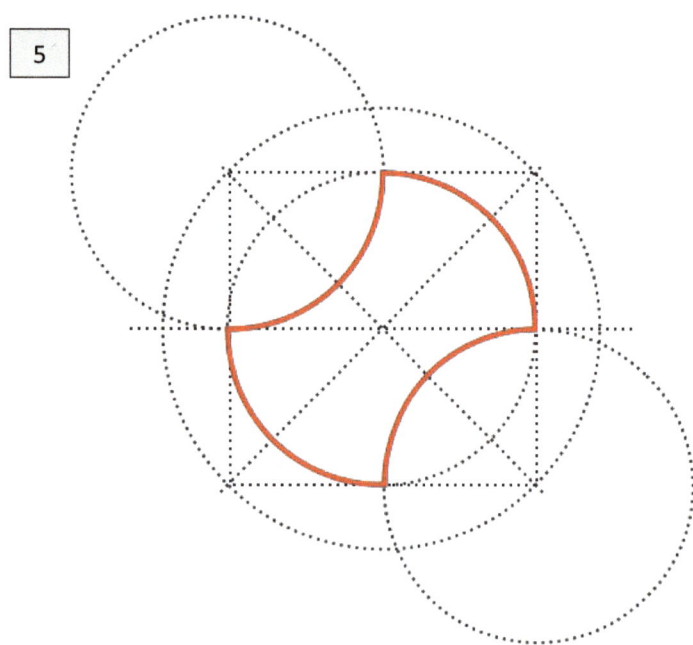

Find this tile tessellating in these circles. (How would you construct this grid pf circles?)

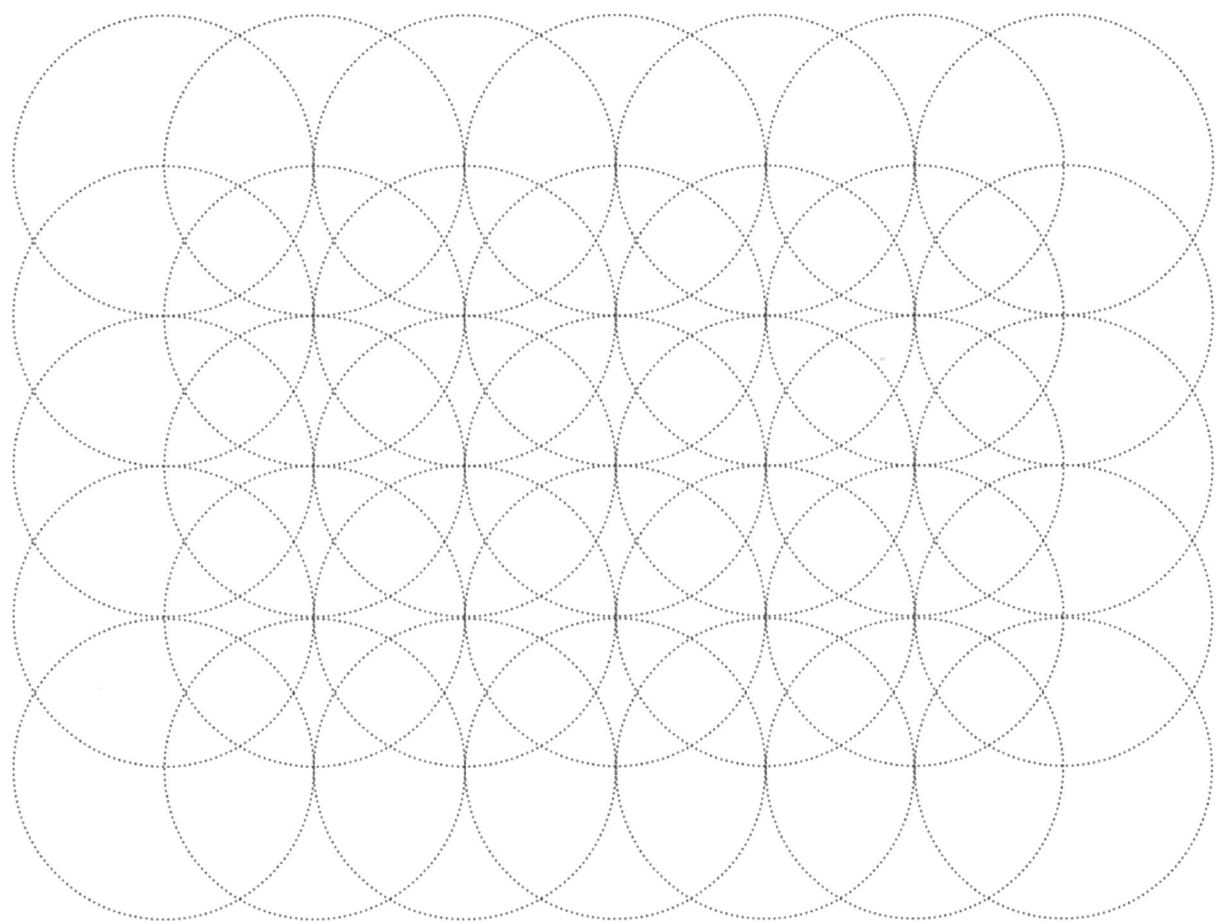

4.

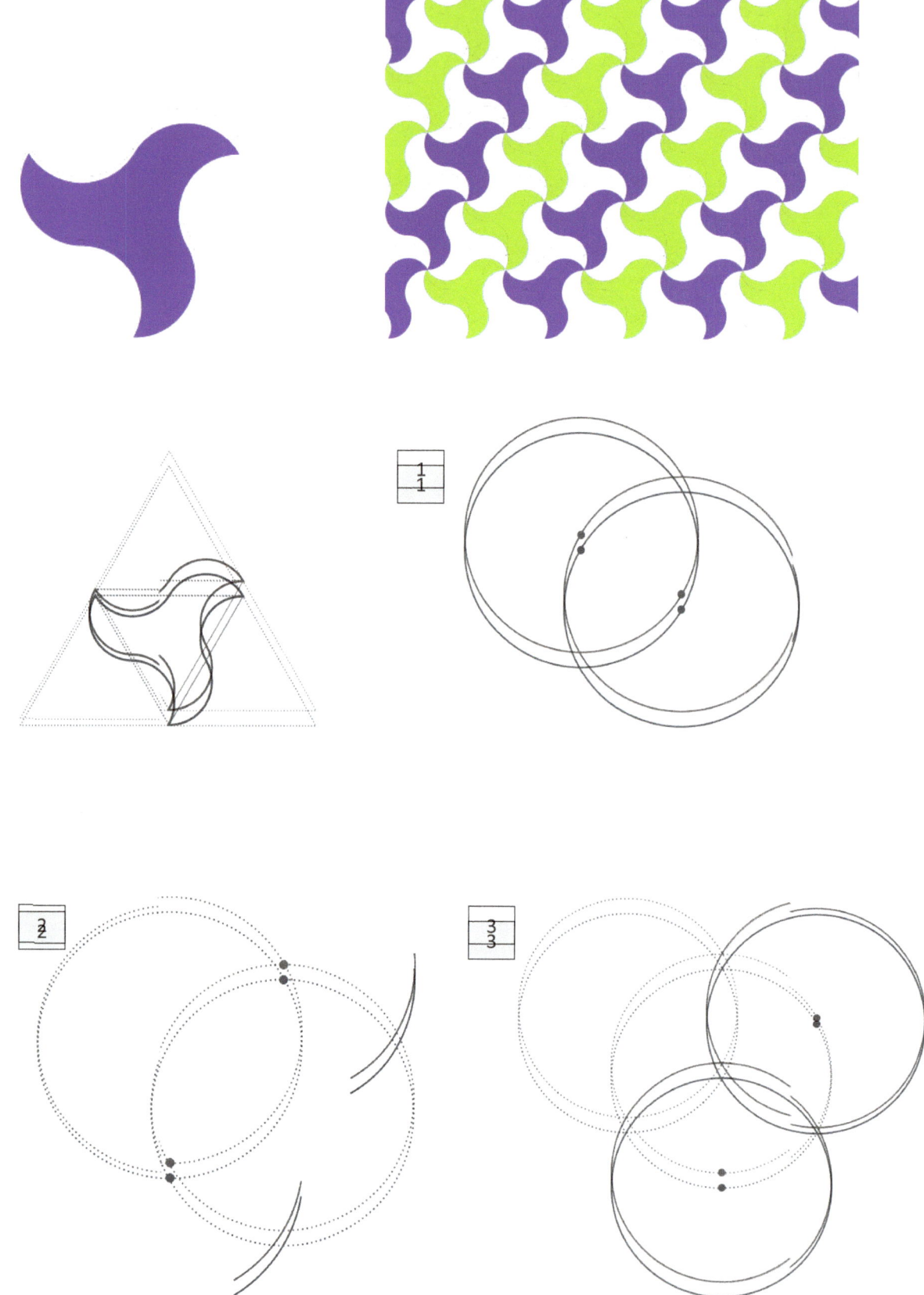

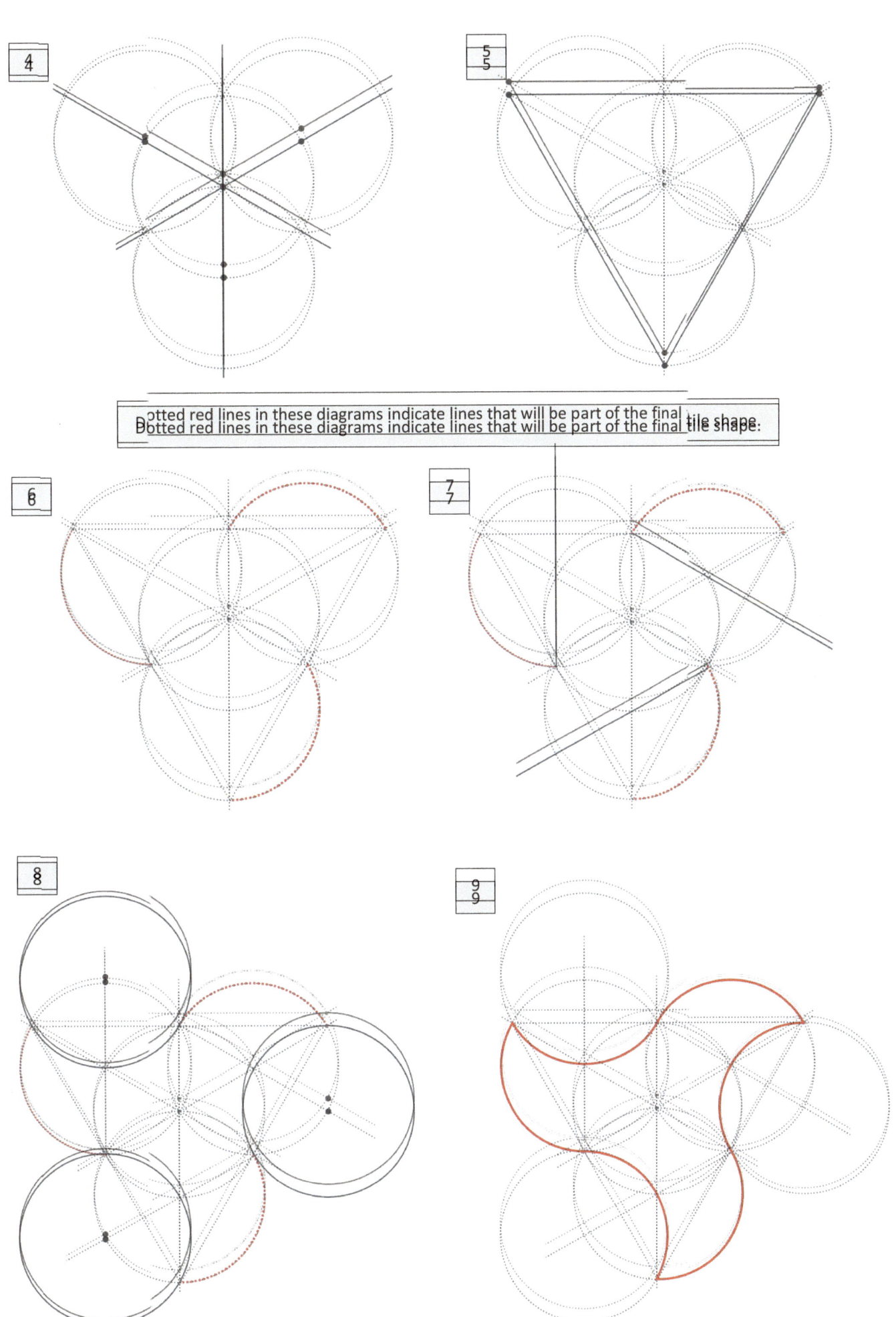

Dotted red lines in these diagrams indicate lines that will be part of the final tile shape:

5.

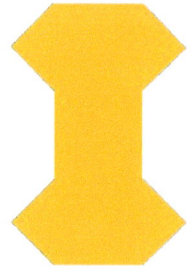
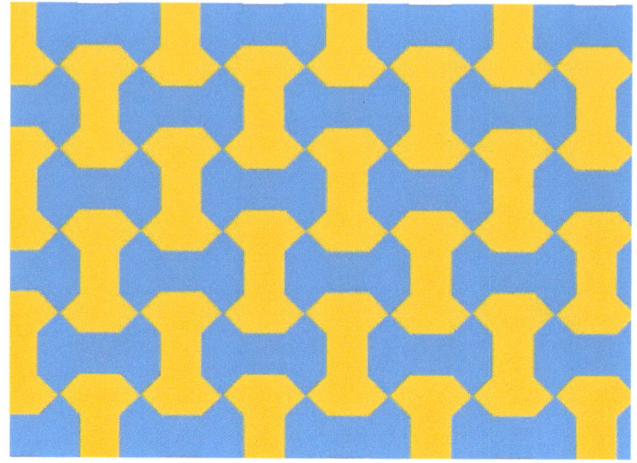

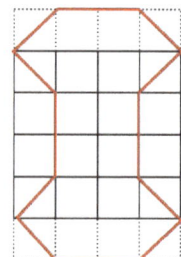

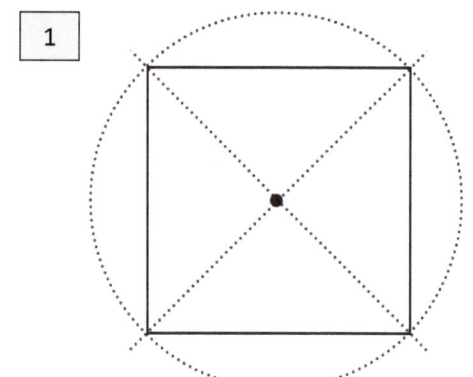
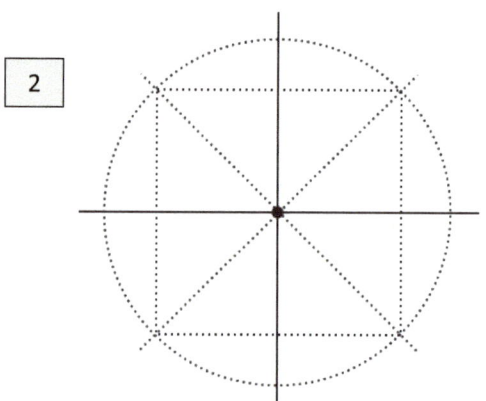

3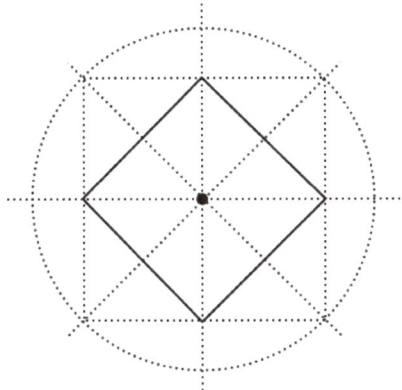

4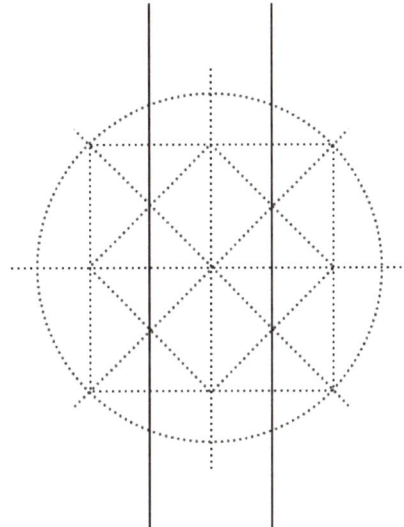

5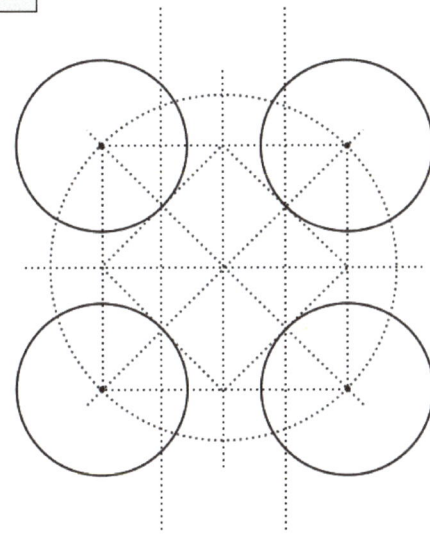

Reset the radius of the compass for these circles.

6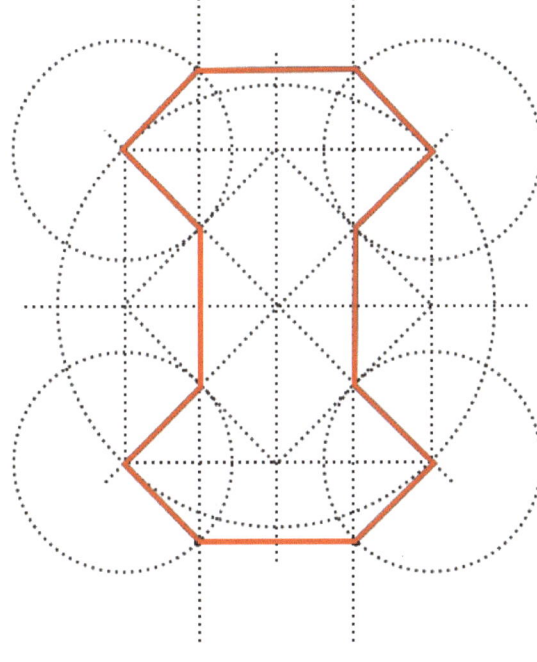

6.

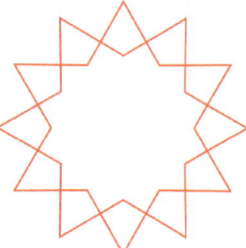
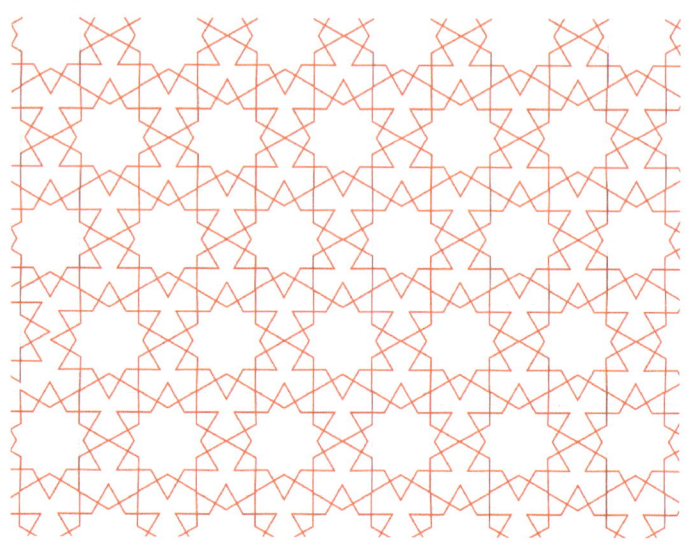

The following two patterns use a different approach. Instead of the 'cut and paste' method, in these patterns a set of guidelines is constructed, and the tessellating shape emerges from these guidelines. In step 2, the centre of the new circle can be any point on the first circle:

1	2
3	4

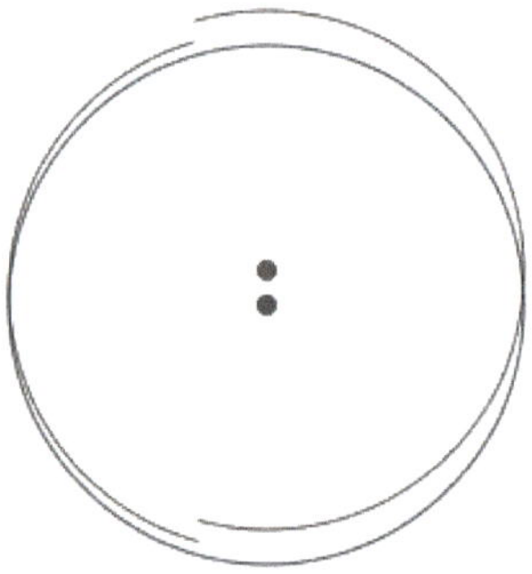

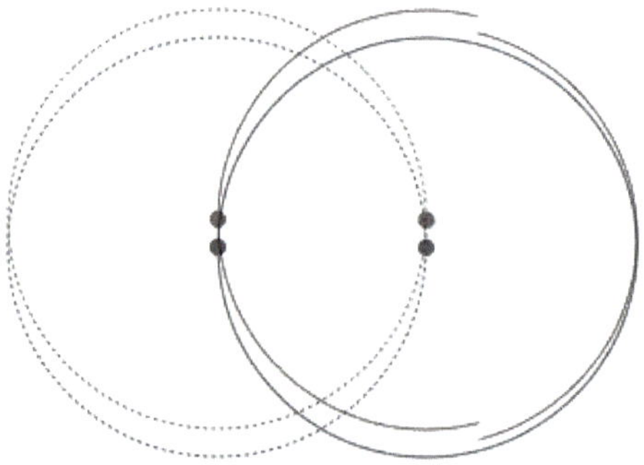

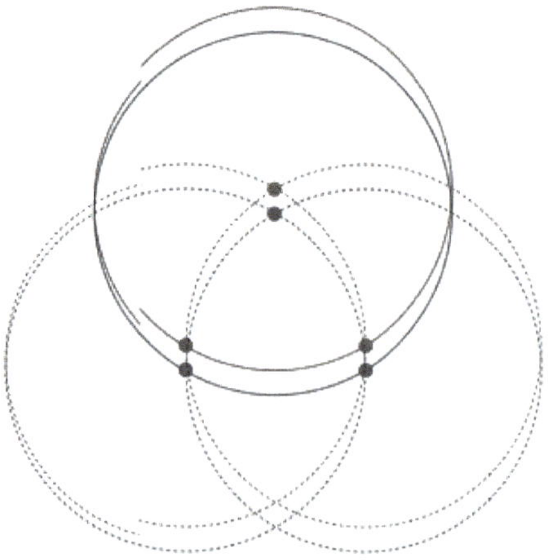

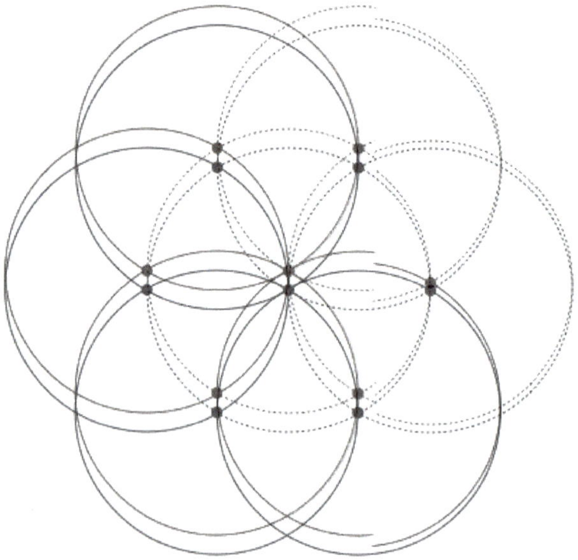

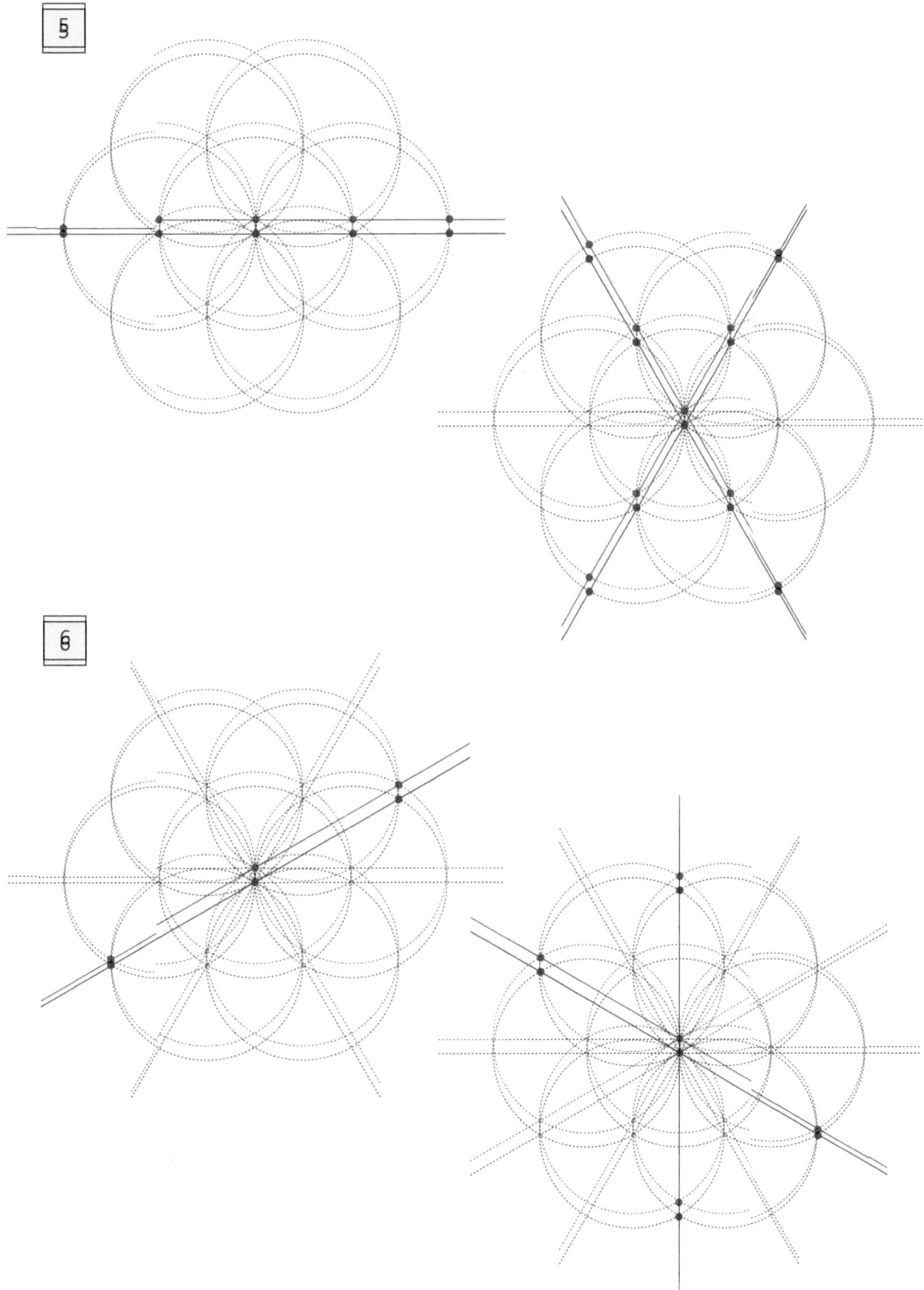

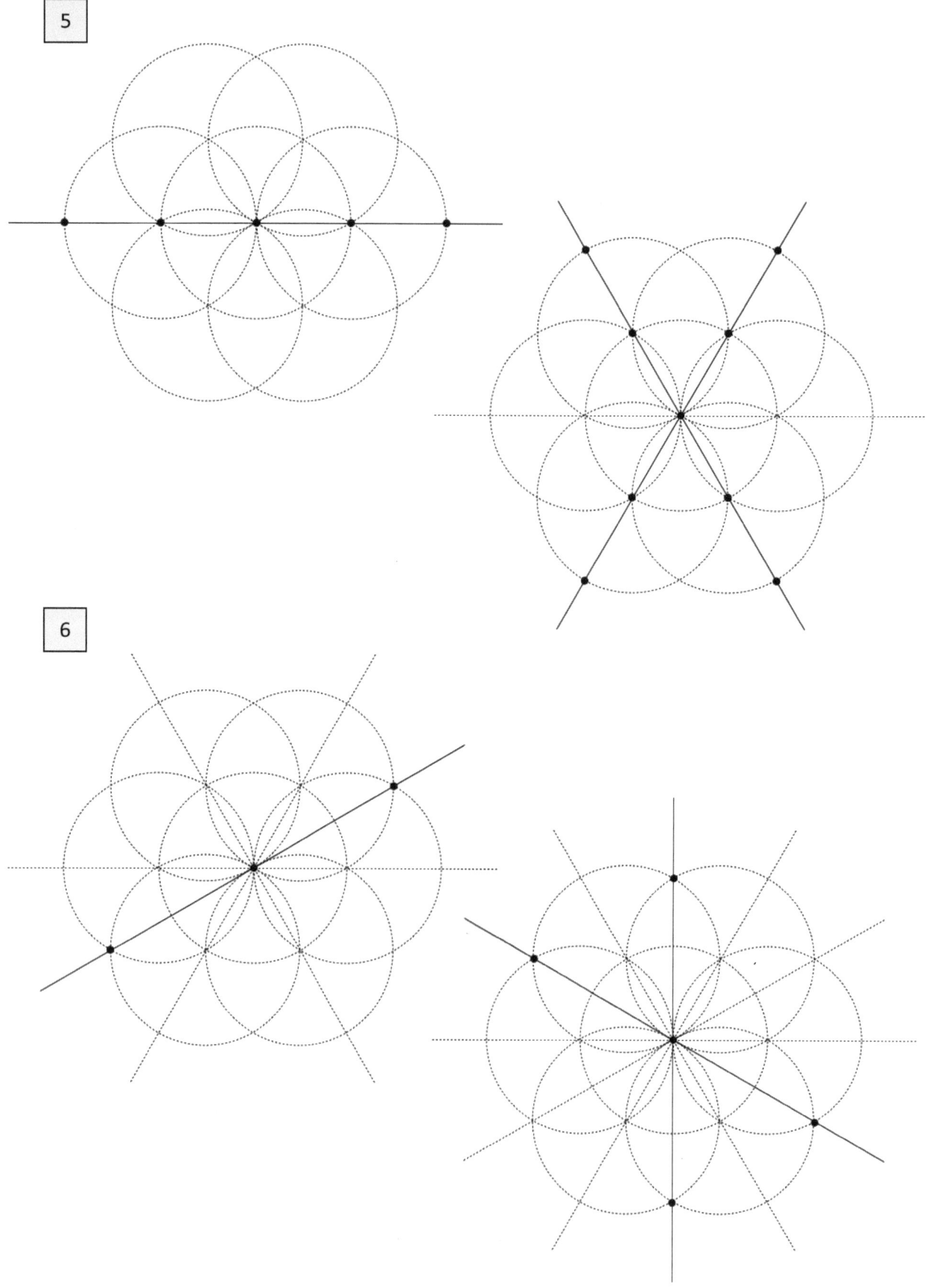

9

10 To make the final pattern, make copies of the star and rotate them by 15°, so that there is a point at the very top.

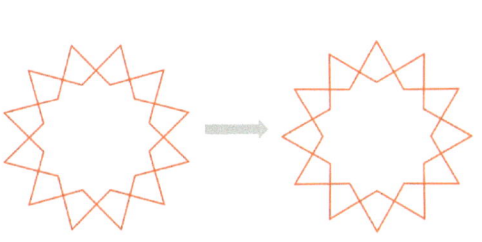

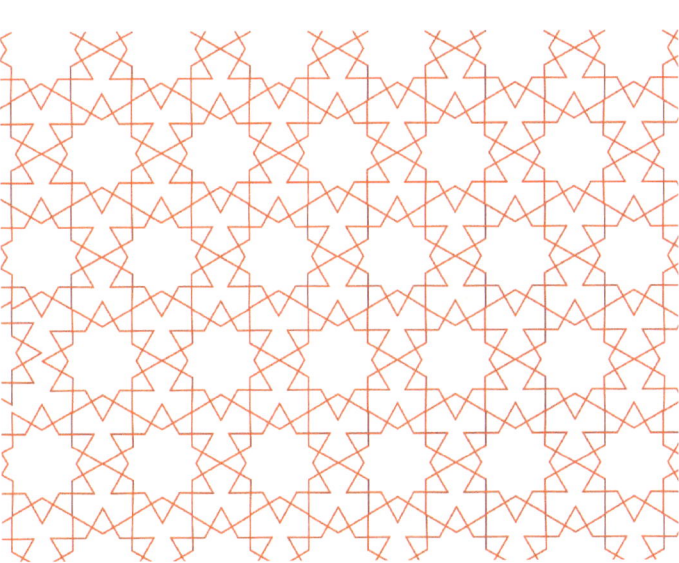

This star can also be tessellated to produce the following pattern:

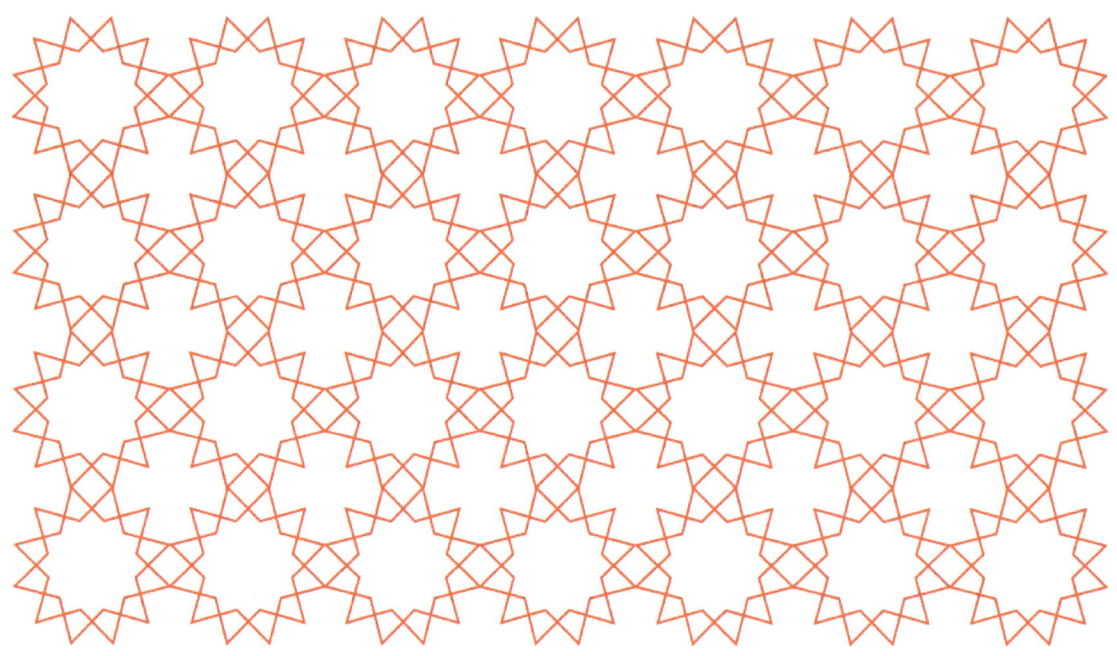

7.

The final Alhambra pattern in this book can be constructed in many ways. This approach introduces a new strategy = overlapping. In this case an octagon is overlapped to produce the final pattern. While this seems to go against the spirit of tessellation, it can make for many beautiful patterns. Once you have made the final pattern, try to identify the tessellating shape within it.

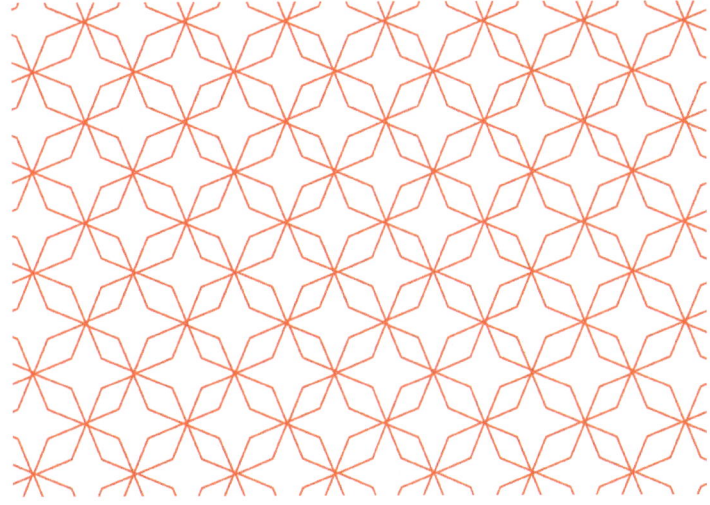

For steps 1 and 2, revise strategies from the beginning of the book.

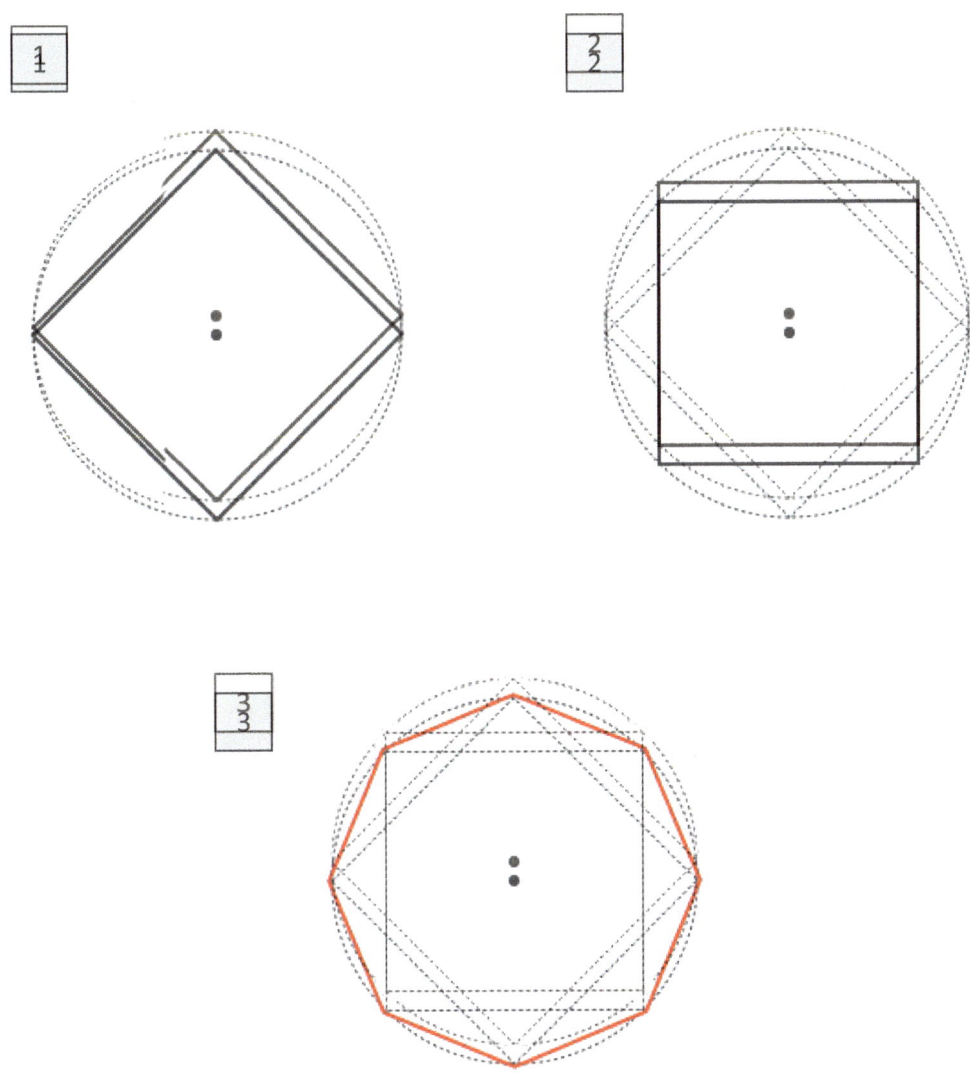

Make a row of octagons:

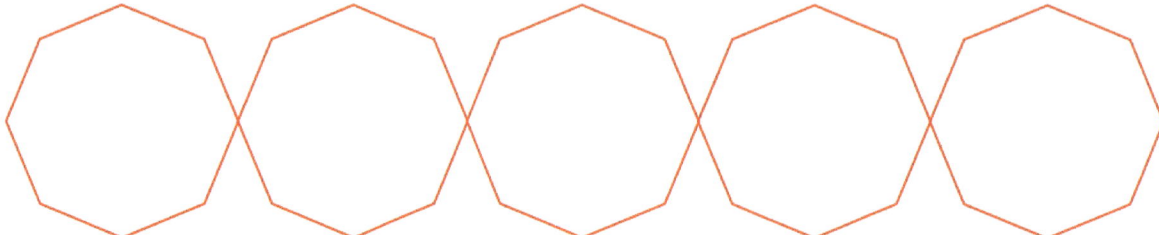

Overlap a second row as follows:

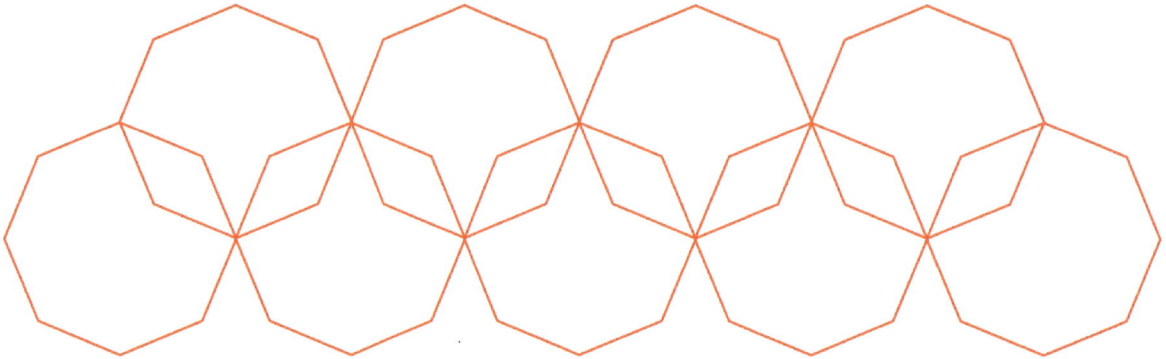

Continue the process to produce the final pattern. Can you find tessellating square units within the pattern?

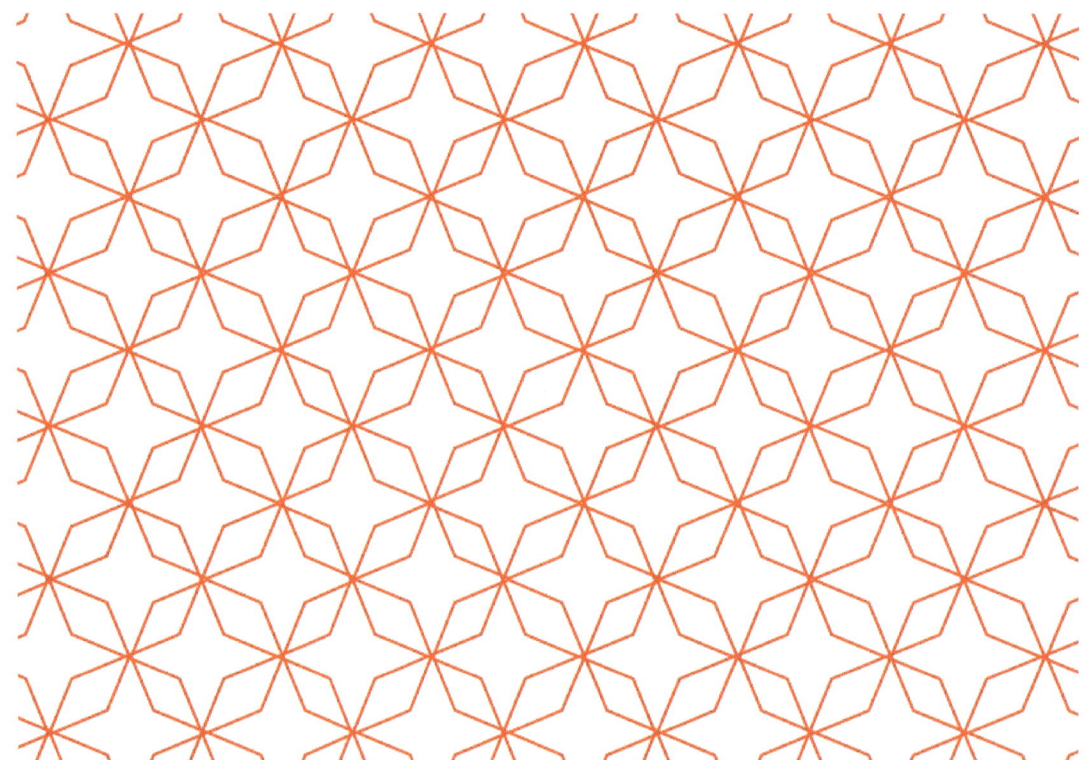

The same pattern can be produced using a four-pointed star as the basic shape. If necessary, review the techniques at the beginning of the book for drawing squares, making right angles, and finding the centre of a line.

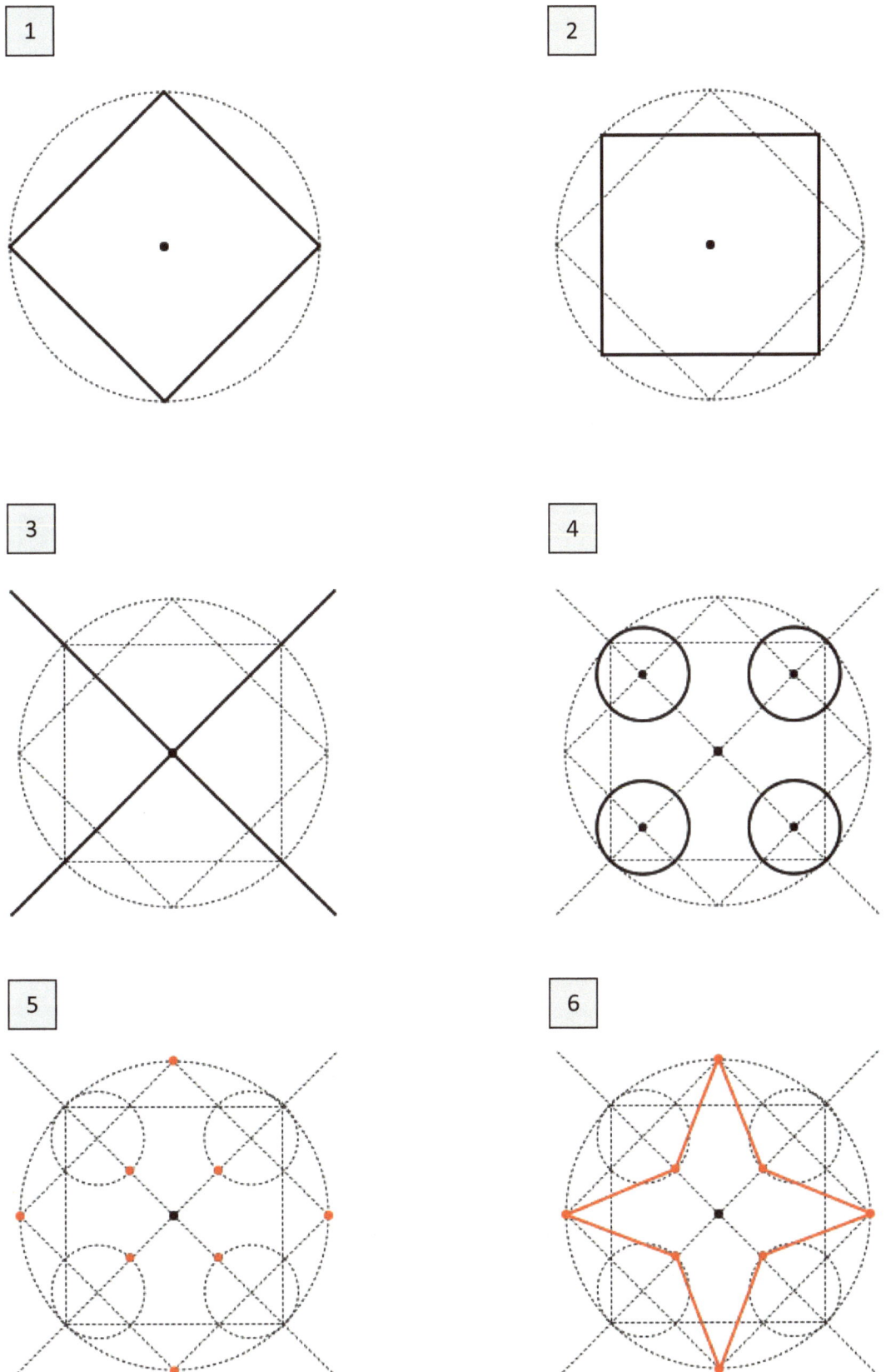

Now the fun really starts. Make copies of the stars and tessellate as shown here:

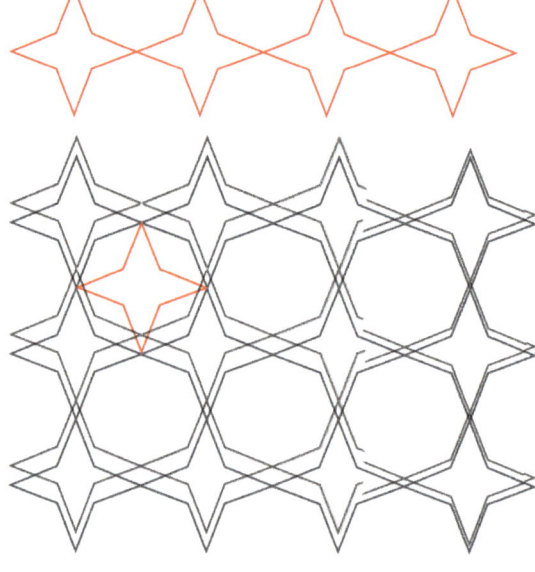

To produce the final pattern, add a star inside each octagon, beginning like this:

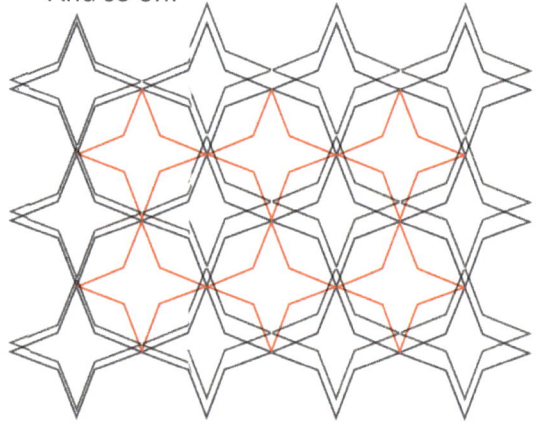

And so on:

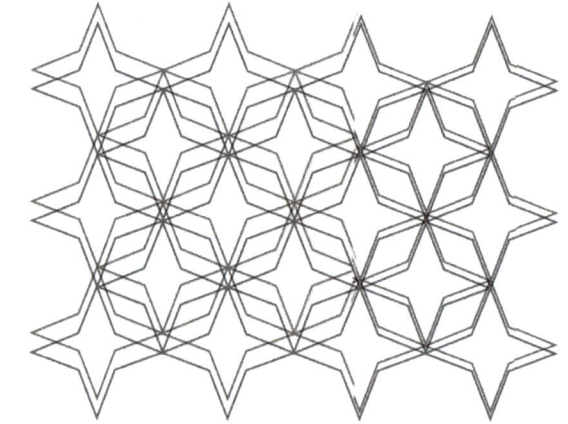

In the Alhambra, the final design is coloured, roughly as follows, and includes shapes inside the stars:

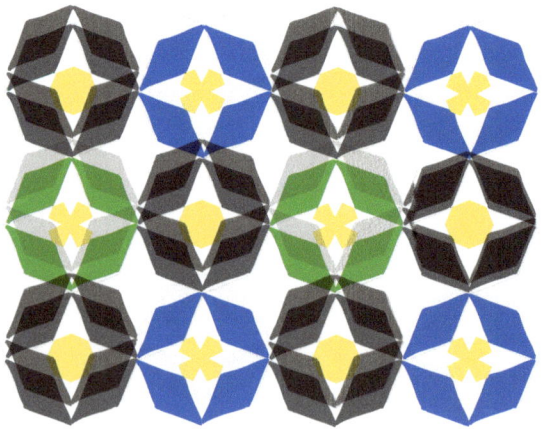

8. Your turn!

These approaches to making patterns can be used to invent new designs. The approach used in the last two patterns is a great place to start. For example, the guidelines produced for the four-pointed star also contain the outline of an eight-pointed star:

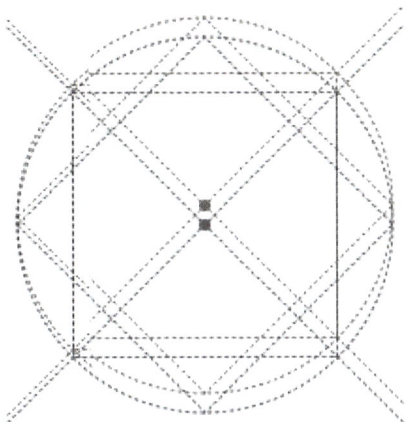 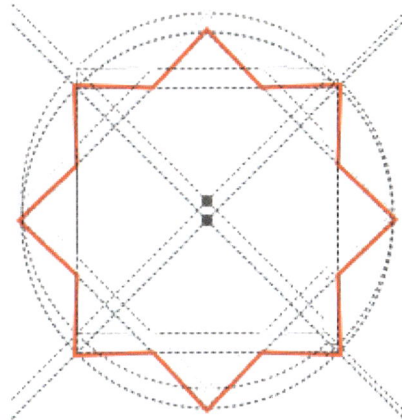

The star can be used to make a range of patterns:

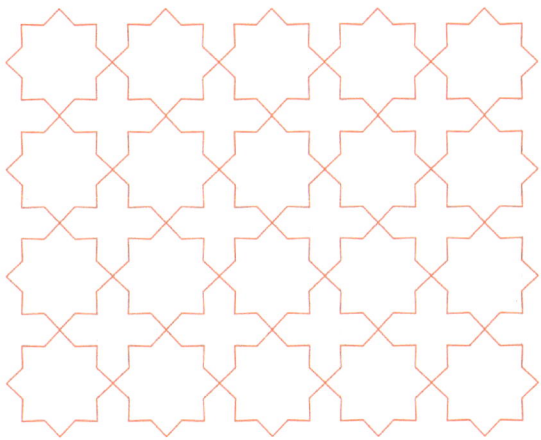 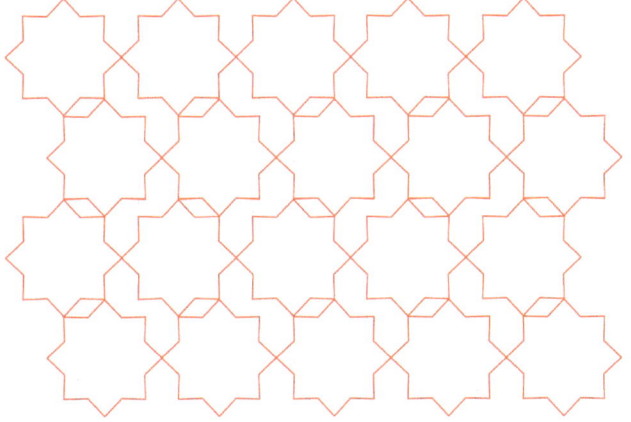

Your turn!

Bonus – The Triquetra

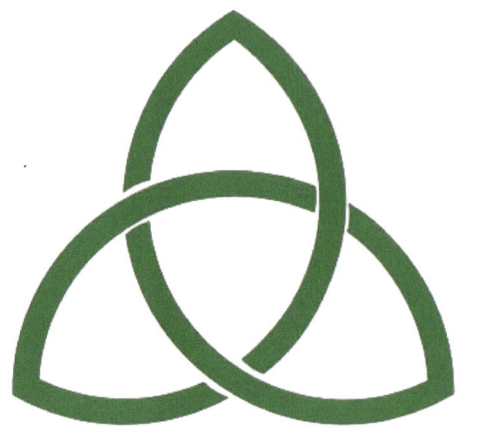

This is not a tessellating tile shape, but a beautiful structure that has been important to many cultures. It can be produced in two ways – the plain version (red), or the interlocking version (green).

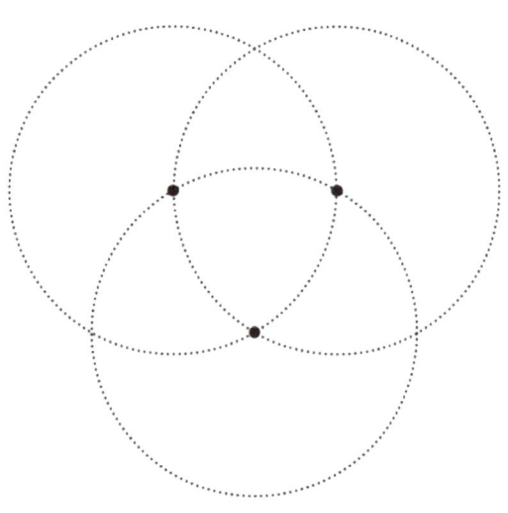
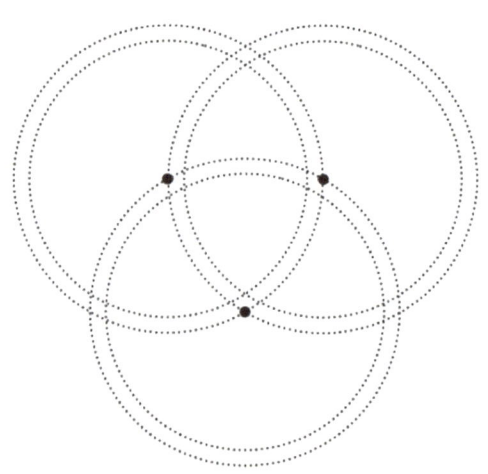
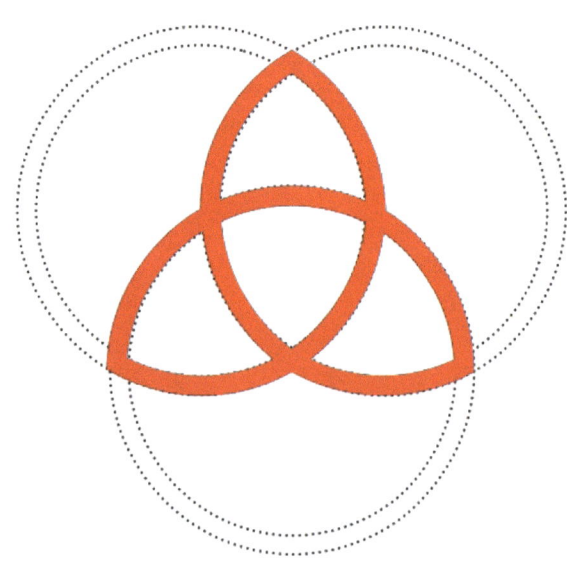
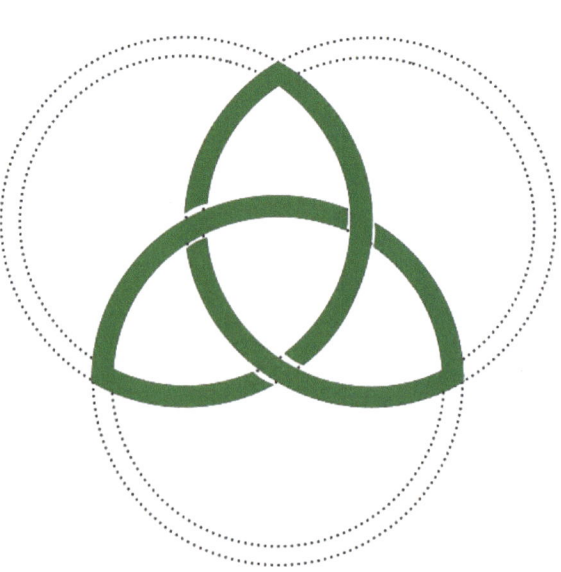

Circles

The following circles may be used as the basis for making tiles in the classroom – if all students begin with circles of the same size, the final tiles can be used to produces a tessellating pattern.

A next step in the process of understanding tessellations is to consider what symmetry transformations are possible with each pattern.

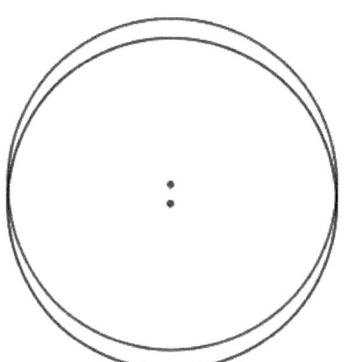

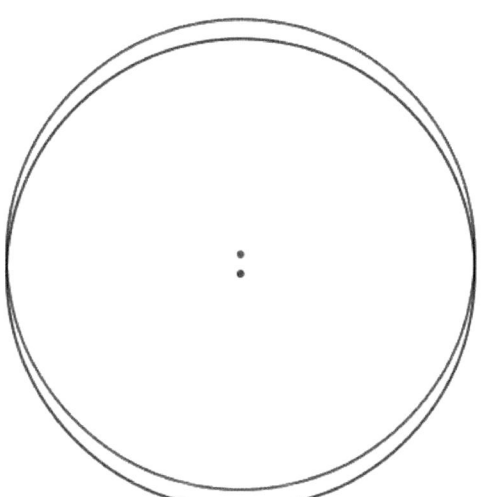

www.ingramcontent.com/pod-product-compliance
Lightning Source LLC
Chambersburg PA
CBHW051941210526
45473CB00006B/2331